Superstars
of the
CHICAGO
CUBS

By Max Hammer

amicus
high interest

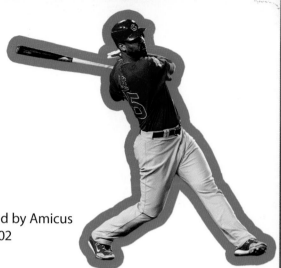

Amicus High Interest is published by Amicus
P.O. Box 1329, Mankato, MN 56002
www.amicuspublishing.us

Library of Congress Cataloging-in-Publication Data
Hammer, Max.
  Superstars of the Chicago Cubs / by Max Hammer.
      p. cm. -- (Pro sports superstars)
  Includes index.
  Summary: "Presents some of the Chicago Cubs' greatest players and
their achievements in pro baseball, including Ryne Sandberg and Starlin
Castro"--Provided by publisher.
  ISBN 978-1-60753-592-8 (hardcover) -- ISBN 978-1-60753-626-0 (pdf
ebook)
  1. Chicago Cubs (Baseball team)--History--Juvenile literature. 2. Baseball
players--United States--History--Juvenile literature. I. Title.
  GV875.C6H37 2014
  796.357'640977311--dc23
                                    2013048645

Photo Credits: Tom DiPace/AP Images, cover; Adam Davis/Icon SMI, 2,
18; Matt York/AP Images, 5; Bettmann/Corbis, 6, 9, 10; Focus on Sport/
Getty Images, 12; Diamond Images/Getty Images, 14; Scott Troyanos/AP
Images, 17, 22; Warren Wimmer/CSR/Icon SMI, 21

Produced for Amicus by The Peterson Publishing Company
and Red Line Editorial.

Editor Arnold Ringstad
Designer Maggie Villaume
Printed in the United States of America
Mankato, MN
9-2014
PO1228
10 9 8 7 6 5 4 3 2

TABLE OF CONTENTS

MEET THE CHICAGO CUBS

The Chicago Cubs have played since 1876. Some say the team is cursed. They have not won a **World Series** since 1908. The Cubs have had many great players. Here are some of the best.

6

MORDECAI BROWN

Mordecai Brown was a great pitcher. He was the team's **ace**. Brown helped the Cubs reach four World Series. The team won two. The last was in 1908.

Mordecai Brown's nickname was "Three Finger." He lost one finger in an accident.

GABBY HARTNETT

Gabby Hartnett was a good catcher. He hit the ball hard too. Hartnett was also great at stealing bases. He won a most valuable player (**MVP**) award in 1935.

9

ERNIE BANKS

Ernie Banks played shortstop and first base. Fans call him "Mr. Cub." He played 19 seasons. All were with the Cubs. Banks won MVP awards in 1958 and 1959.

Ernie Banks loved baseball. He sometimes said, "Let's play two!"

BILLY WILLIAMS

Billy Williams played left field. He was shy. But he was a great hitter. Williams hit 426 **home runs** in his career. He had the best **batting average** in 1972.

14

RON SANTO

Ron Santo was a great third baseman. He was only the second player at his position to hit 300 home runs. Santo retired in 1974. He joined the **Hall of Fame** in 2012.

The Cubs' stadium has a statue of Santo.

RYNE SANDBERG

Ryne Sandberg was a skilled hitter. He hit two home runs in one game in 1984. He was also a great fielder. Sandberg won nine **Gold Glove Awards**.

Sandberg later became a manager for the Philadelphia Phillies.

17

DERREK LEE

Derrek Lee played first base. He had a great year in 1995. He won the batting title. This meant he had the highest batting average. He also won a Gold Glove Award that year.

Lee spent time in Japan as a boy. His father played baseball there.

STARLIN CASTRO

Starlin Castro is a speedy shortstop. He joined the team at age 20. Castro played in the **All-Star Game** in 2011.

The Cubs have had many great superstars. Who will be next?

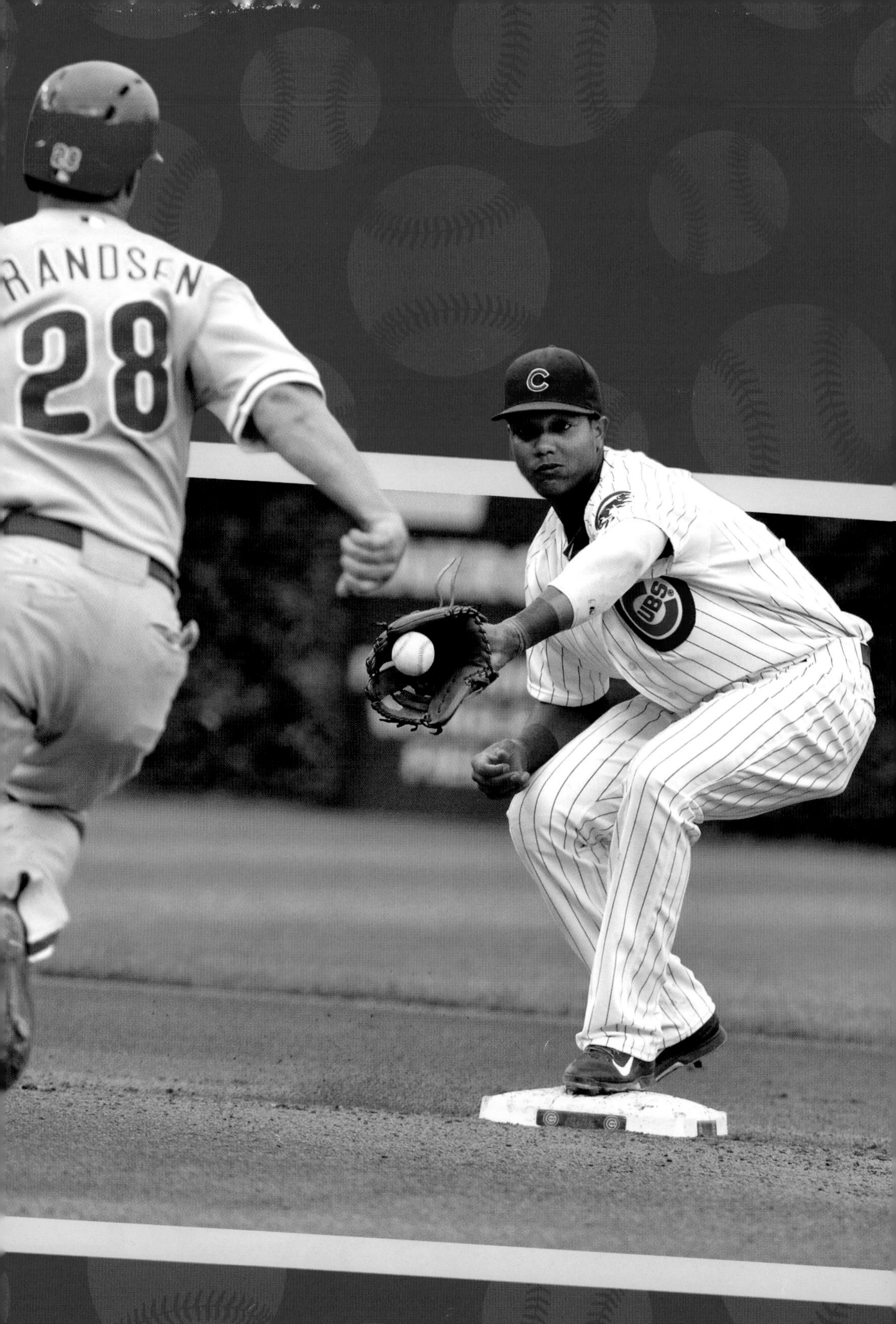
RANDSEN
28

TEAM FAST FACTS

Founded: 1876

Other names: Chicago White Stockings (1876–1889), Chicago Colts (1890–1897), Chicago Orphans (1898–1901)

Nicknames: Cubbies, the Lovable Losers

Home Stadium: Wrigley Field (Chicago, Illinois)

World Series Championships: 2 (1907 and 1908)

Hall of Fame Players: 42, including Ryne Sandberg, Ron Santo, Billy Williams, Ernie Banks, Mordecai Brown, and Gabby Hartnett (also 15 managers)

WORDS TO KNOW

ace – the best starting pitcher on a given team

All-Star Game – a game between the best players in baseball each year

batting average – a number that tells how often a player hits the ball and reaches base

Gold Glove Awards – awards given to the best fielders each year

Hall of Fame – a group of baseball players honored as the best ever

home runs – hits that go far enough to leave the field, letting the hitter run all the way around the bases to score a run

MVP – Most Valuable Player; an honor given to the best player each season

World Series – the annual baseball championship series

LEARN MORE

Books

Castle, George. *Chicago Cubs (Inside MLB)*. Minneapolis, MN: Abdo, 2011.

Gilbert, Sara. *Chicago Cubs*. Mankato, MN: Creative Education, 2013.

Web Sites

Baseball History
http://mlb.mlb.com/mlb/history
Learn more about the history of baseball.

Chicago Cubs—Official Site
http://chicago.cubs.mlb.com
Watch video clips and read stories about the Chicago Cubs.

MLB.com
http://mlb.com
See pictures and track your favorite baseball player's stats.

INDEX